The Lightworkers

The Lightworkers

Incantations to Awaken Utopia
from Within

by Madiha Bee

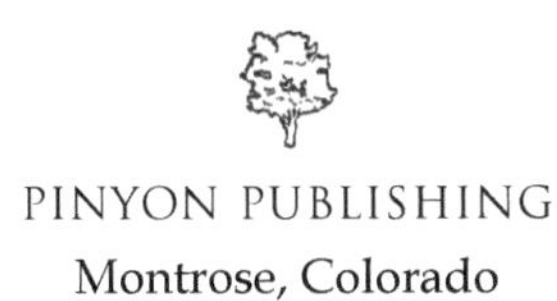

PINYON PUBLISHING
Montrose, Colorado

Copyright © 2020 by Madiha Bee

All rights reserved. Except as permitted under the U.S. Copyright Act of 1976, no part of this publication may be reproduced, distributed, or transmitted in any form or by any means, or stored in a database or retrieval system, without the prior written permission of the publisher, except for brief quotations in articles, books, and reviews.

Madiha Bee on Facebook & Instagram: @madihabeecoaching

Invitations, readings, and questions via e-mail:
madihabeecoaching@gmail.com

Art by Madiha Bee

Cover Photograph of Madiha Bee by Salah Salem

Design by Shamas Bedi & Susan Entsminger

First Edition: April 2020

Pinyon Publishing
23847 V66 Trail, Montrose, CO 81403
www.pinyon-publishing.com

Library of Congress Control Number: 2020932285
ISBN: 978-1-936671-61-8

For Ehab,

my love, my best friend, my ally,

for loving the poetry inside me

and believing in my dreams.

And for my readers,

that we might remember together

a much holier world than we were ever told existed.

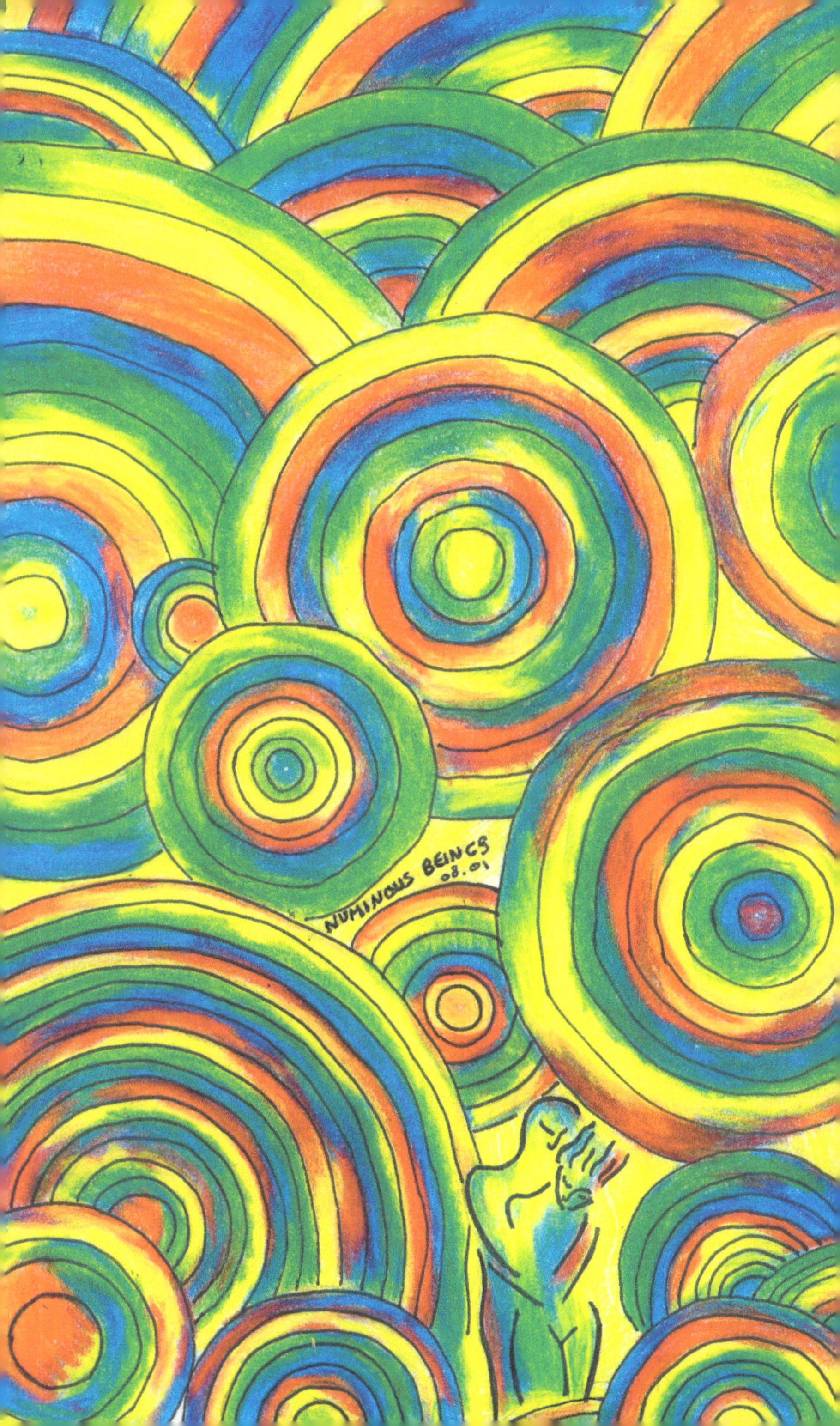
NUMINOUS BEINGS
08.01

Inside this Collection

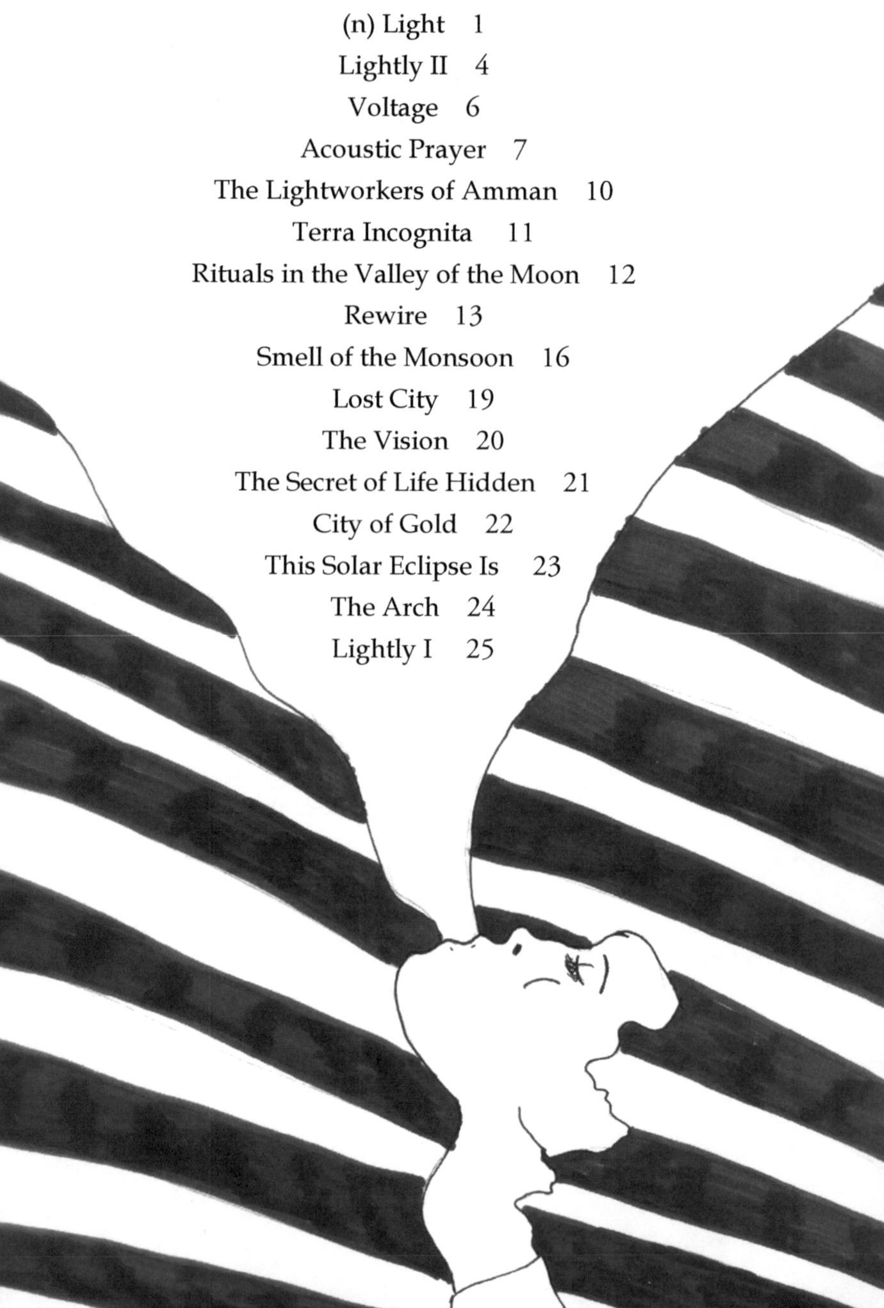

(n) Light

was the first word
added to my
slowly accumulating more

fingers pointing to the soft
of mother's cheek
I couldn't say, but

light grew
when the wide of sky was paper white
when cotton blanket wrapped

around
in the
night

when first stolen sight of my sister brought
morning
in that squinting, searching, Northstar of a face

light
against backdrop of the old unknown and black box trunks
and the whale of a womb

against tremors,
a young planet's fear
ofthetideofeyes

smooth
against clamor   of snow turbulent and the takeoff
of flight

light
like revelation waiting above
the wing of clouds

and the flirting waves of tarried notes,
an inner reflective
screamed aloud

something of that light
rolls
down

like the downpour of love for a newly born
just fallen
from the sky

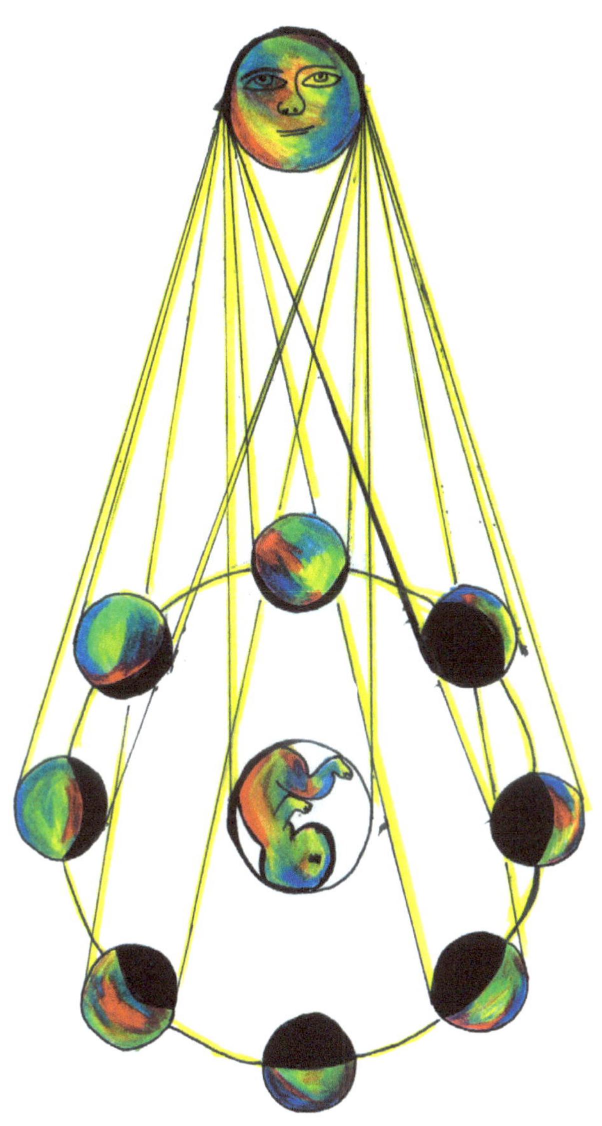

Lightly II

the priestess stood by a wide-worn window
wiping clean the thin of leaves,
an island fur of entrance plants
showership of light and krypton sighs,
    the crib and nave of a numinous rhythm
green hands receiving waterwings and sun, gathering
    paradise
                            recalling time as a ceremonial
                            ancient where air travels   far,
speeds in space and minutes towards no   end
                        a white flag on a high-floor
                        crossroad
                            on a city hill
                            on a map on a planetary turn
stroking shoulders and sides like sea
                            oracles of soft and skin,
emerald sleeves in the ritual of the stroke,
in a guardian's deep and tendered
    offering of knowledge,   of baring sacred   what is most
    knowing
of body temperatures and the harbor
of gentleness   and   the soil.

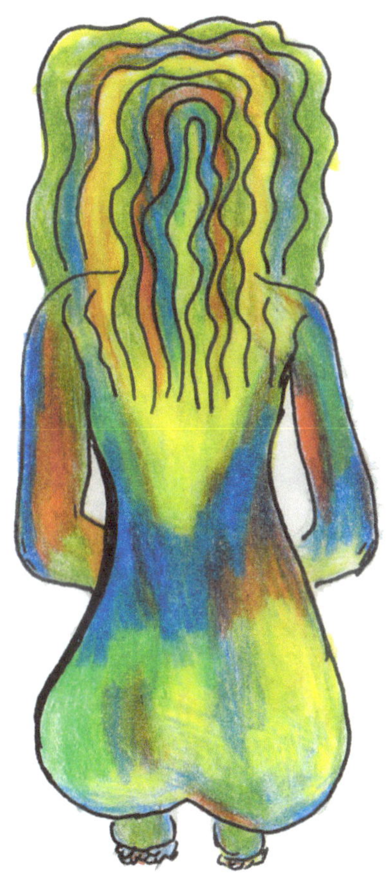

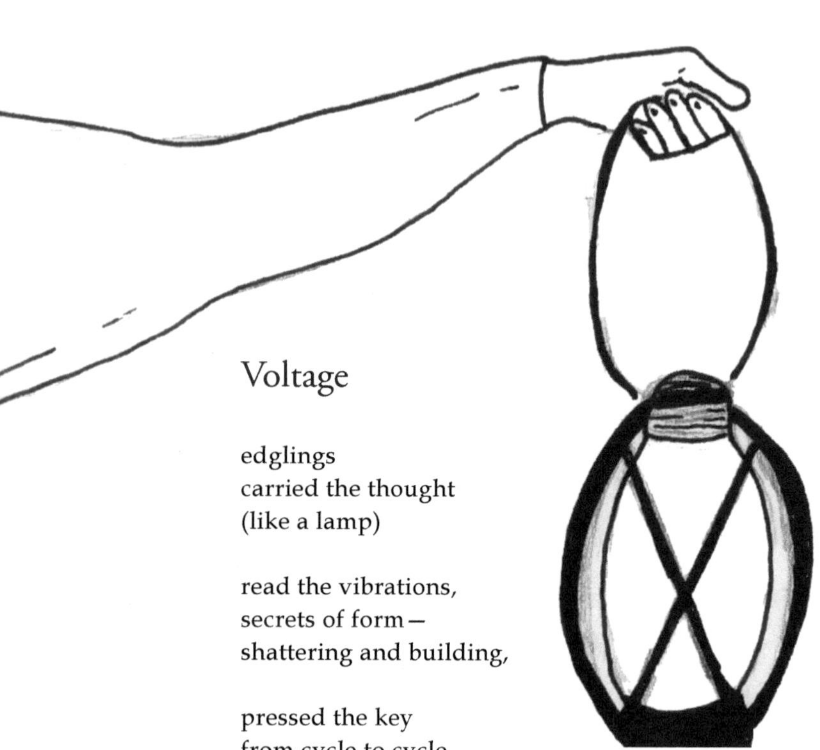

Voltage

edglings
carried the thought
(like a lamp)

read the vibrations,
secrets of form—
shattering and building,

pressed the key
from cycle to cycle
of roads electric

to higher—*I am that*
I am and there is
nought else: the brightness

inside sleeps
until the water breaks
and light precipitates,

streaming into our sun
systems, force currents,
dynamic impulse and a whole

clear channel for the passage
of senses
and solar rays.

Acoustic Prayer

I want to be more
humble as a bumble bee
green as the royal gardens

sacred as the prophet's belt
cosmic and minute
as a breath

or snowed in
as a blade of grass or a song that climbs the skin
and curls inside the throat

but one thing stands in
the way:
delusional enough to think I can be

only one thing
at a time
when life unfolds and the mantle is just

a layer
slumbering under the shade
of a tree.
I want to go where the ants dance out the
morning madness, mouth the
depths of matter,

untie the double
helix, lick
the wounds holy inside the atoms, burning

everything unnecessary
to discover the true murmur of the heart: one
look at this moment and we unravel, only colors

of *now* remain,
bathing the air of battles
with the scripture of where we started

when sand and smoke met
for the first
time,

the incantation of a stormy sea,
the forward drift of the ride
back home.

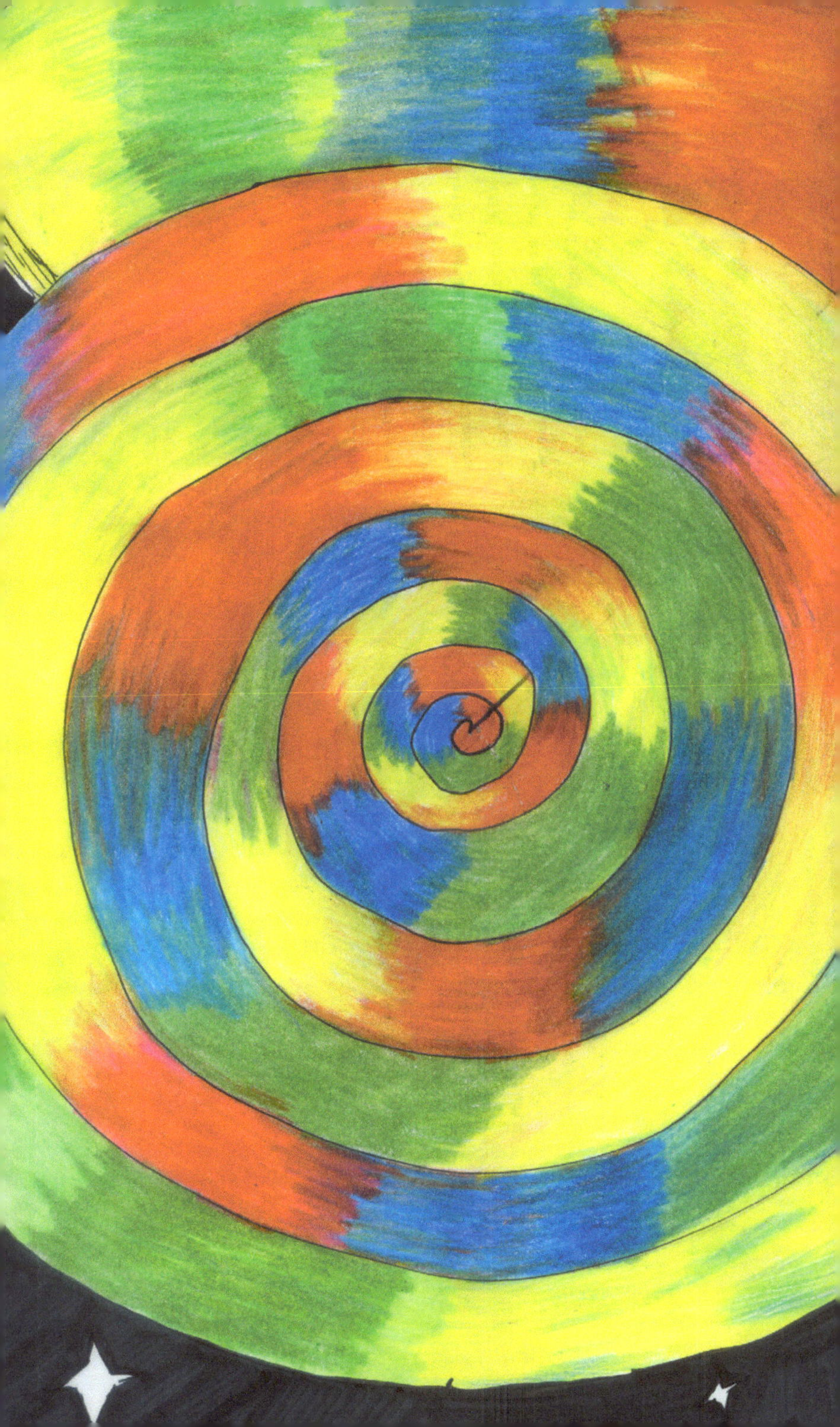

The Lightworkers of Amman

The concrete ground cracked open city hall
and we wondered whether falling
in would be the paper path,
to build and sculpt the emotive structures
from inside out
from foundations up
from bones of land and body and mines,
to stretches of rooftop minds and high
this s k y-c l o s e sound, a light geometry,
vibration of the unknown mass
budding affinities   crepuscular and spiraling
like a procession   a litany of wildness
an oration of the corybantic cell (unpeeled and rib cage
charged with spark) holy perfume that flutters
round and round the circle   twelve hundred eyes
precious like
diamonds,   dreaming up the Movement of Okay.
Things will be okay.
The air will clear.

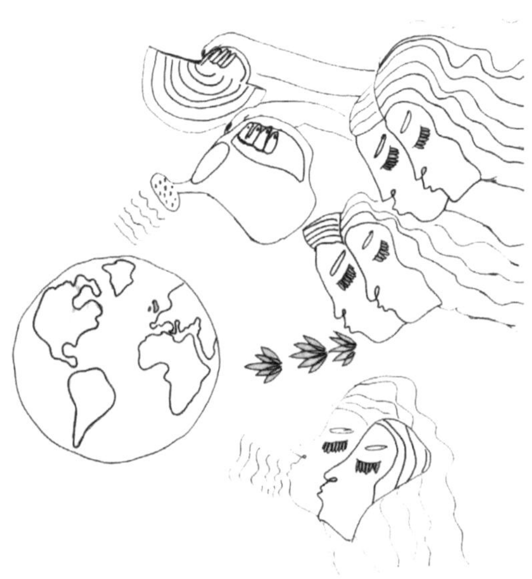

Terra Incognita

I stop to read the language of the earth herself, to lose myself,
knowing exactly where I am   finding another way home,
stepping into a   realm not yet mapped,

a pulse of discovery in the vastness,
the sweet strangeness of the world ahead,
unraveling in a million moments of arrival.

How will you go about finding
that thing the nature of which is
totally unknown to you?

Rituals in the Valley of the Moon

Teach us to whisper into the ears of strangers
into bodies that mirror the breathing sands
breezed in the mellow of a night's red-yellow
to listen to the giving of a word
its carrying and luxurious offering

velvet blanketeer of human adoration,   shapeshifter
of the dunes   beat that dissolves the mirage, loosens our
    scorpion screws—
the receiver is blind-folded and the scholar, asleep, leaning on
a coffee-colored camel-seat, a dream-like falling
towards the earth of a glossary of fevers where the sleepy
    heart awakens in a fire

  m   v   n
      o   i   g   between worlds (when one is clearly
broken beyond repair):
a pause   and listening   to whispers saying:
you are loved,
you are kind,
you are worthy.

Rewire

My people have it going
in happiness they say
may you be blessed (sure)
may you bury me (no thanks)
and sometimes in death:
may the rest of him live on
in you,

what can breathe from under this earth? Spring was a reason to say
I met the Manna tribe in May, moon mystics
who blew sea strings into the smoke above pyres
and called out to the genius of mountains where
rocks once harder than words when they are funereal
became breakable,
sudden and steady, dancing like orbiting planets,
calling names into the phosphorescence
and the darkest Kali
pointed deserts with streams drifting underneath
so bodies piled on bodies and the songs of the night
revealed their star-filled hearts, drew Orion onto the dunes,
swam in anthems of mantra
and embrace,
marching waves to water the edges of a tribal tradition,
carving ways to break mountains with kindness and the milk
of wilding affections, echo
rewiring a compass of affiliations from within, without losing
pulse   of the Bedouin heart
of the land
rewire
for sweet mist breakfasts of soft eyes and high-scape confessionals,
for mercy madness and more
rewire
for thundering sounds that echo from the rosy-ribbed coves,
for city-wolves that howl at the slumbering nights,
echo
rewire

for true nature seen in these beginnings
echo
rewire
for truth revealed
rewire

some tribes have it going
in happiness, and in death, they say
let us be true.

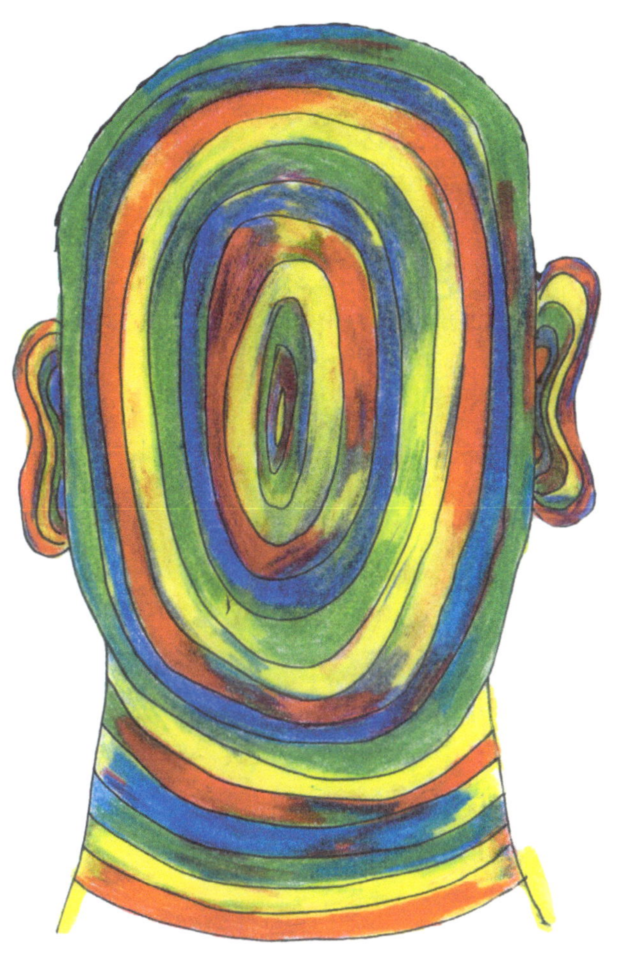

Smell of the Monsoon

Listen to the ancient hum
recreating the earthy
aroma of first rains

acacia, syrian rue
roots and pure rose
a subtle (yet ambrosial)

steam distillation, suspending
flowers over searing water,
a sealed container, a vessel,

bamboo pipes and jasmine, kewra,
mitti, or gill (wet earth) she laughs,
you already smell of the monsoon.

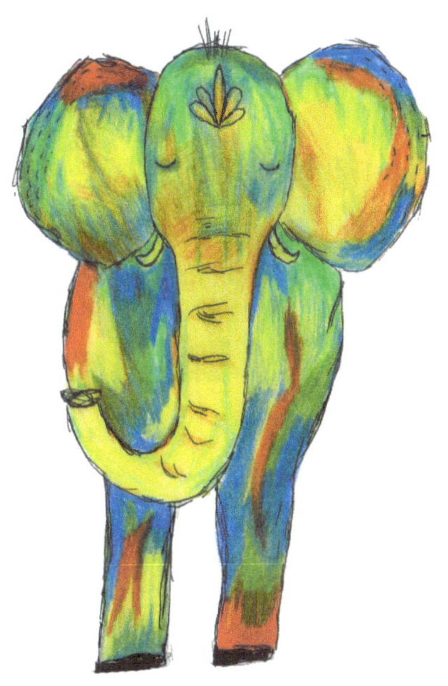

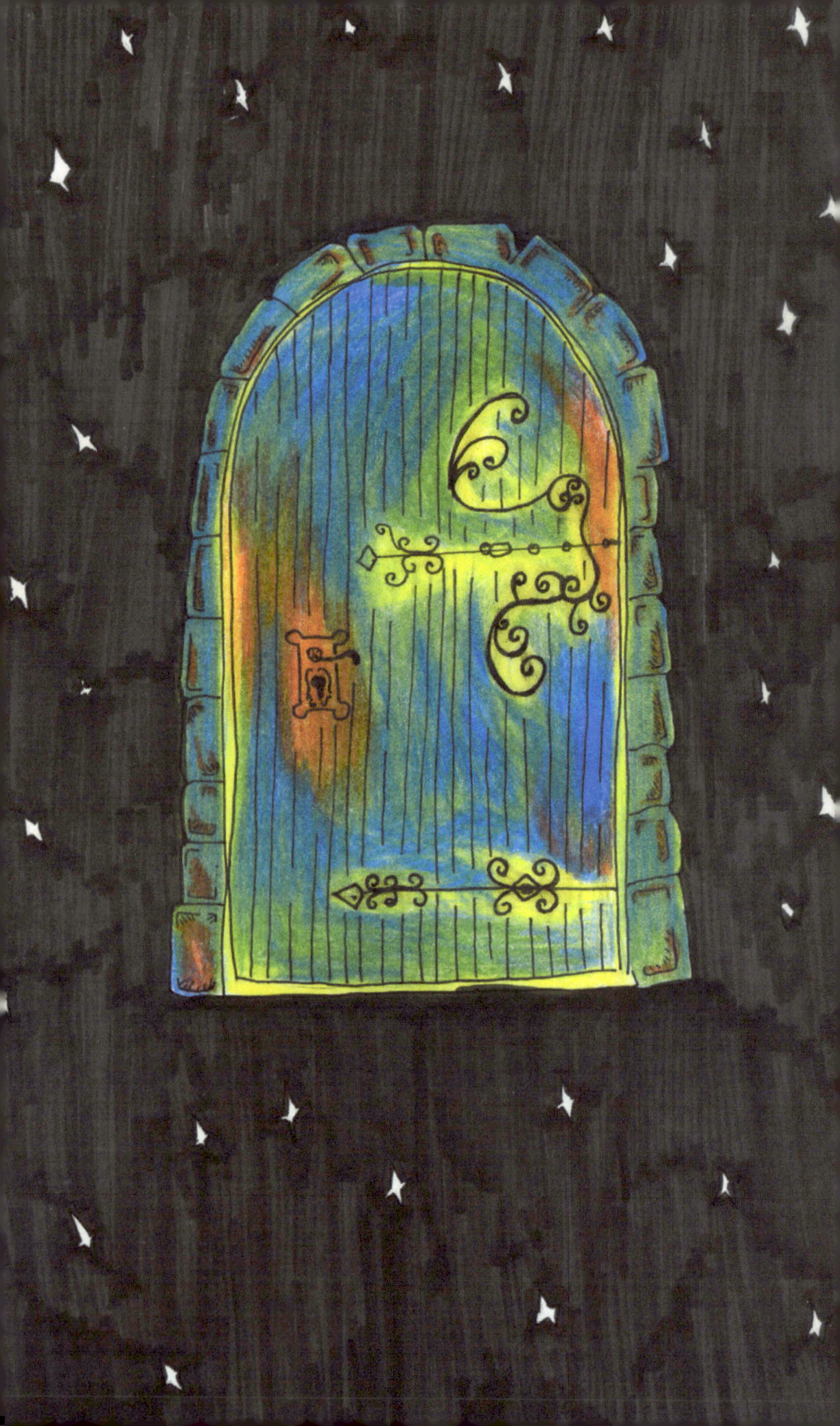

Lost City

preserved by electrification
(you don't see its light until you enter
the dramatic, vertical landscape) the bottom
of a valley where rivers meet
receiving floods (& gold minds)

not the biggest gorge of its kind
but one that contains a flash, secrets eroded,
granite silvered with art that roars, the center
of a temple, a world apart; wildlife, hydraulics,
acoustics—mirrors that make the water dance.

The Vision

aligned with the extreme rising
of mountains dressed in sun capes,
hear the Humpback's migration
I exist at the moment I crash
into you, grave sea that claws the ceilings off stars,
unleashes pioneering waves—this cycle of
the moon,   white and unwritten upon, find me
in the lips of light   as night sips
north to south, signals
the magic of the mangrove root
when was the last time you fell so free?
spine-thunder the spirit   here
where the disfigured turn cinders into spark.

The Secret of Life Hidden

in caves, seeds incipient
do not go in there, out
curiosity tugs at the hollow
this is something to see

find pearl alterations
what lies buried in
the sounds (not tectonic
but gentler still) bordered
by cliff, seeped into

crevice, heard below
the twirling, monkey
shoulders of rivers trickling
beyond the bay, a recollection
by the coast, riding unicycles five feet

tall,
licking ice
from inside
the cosmic
rock.

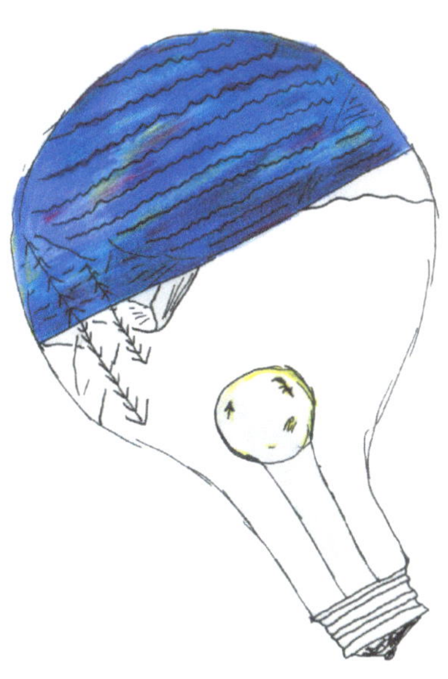

City of Gold

Her buildings are bathed a golden hue
mingling among temples,
traders' wooden homes
a paleness that absorbs less

heat, even her streets, canals
and bridges breathe alters
in yellow ornament
and oils, dedicated orison

to the departed, weaving early solar
into morning,   bouncing off
walls, a tapestry
of light, the back of homes opening

onto sea, easing the load
of goods   and the few noises you hear,
the sweeping of brooms: a brush
of tendered care for all that is living.

This Solar Eclipse Is

spectacular   it moves
the world upside

n w o d. the moon blocks the sun
and in the middle of the day we notice

stars, the sun's corona, solar flickers
burning our aches with their stillness.

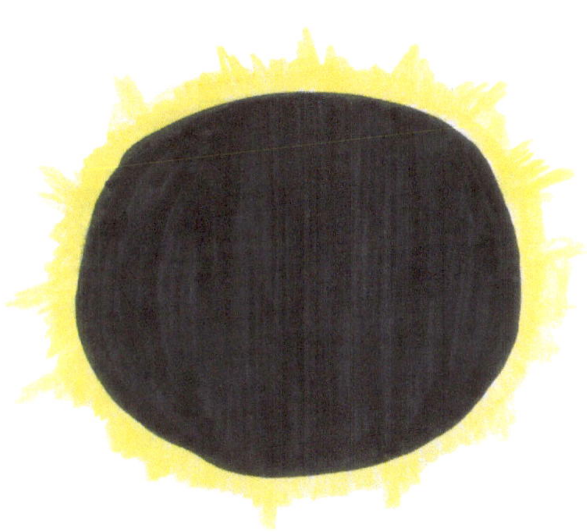

The Arch

In the womb of the vast middle
east disaster zone, we built the world's
largest moving heart structure to prevent
radiation spewing from nuclear sites
    the   slumbering
ink-dried sun recited:

this spell will be a start.

Now trees sprout from the rusted pipes and crumbling
roofs, a new wonder splashes through the windows,
holds the house of nuclear meltdown close.
The arch covers the site, closes in on the outflow.
Reactors dismantle when we wake up far
from that dimmed dimension:

this is the most important work we have ever done.

The zone remains uninhabitable, closed to visitors,
but branches reach for the expanse/an open surgery
(or evolution) to find space for lighter definitions
of the daylight's flow,
an utterance about the strangeness of the new clear mind
an opening of questions like

what have you felt so deeply?

Lightly I

between the silicon swerving of an ibis,
reflecting retinas of a royal sun,
and the silent note sounding of the cicada bug,
stuffed head-deep
in a sunk of land,
I am trying to hold in the lightly
of spoor and steps
the codes of thin   like hiccup segments
the weightless coke float city or hotspot of the heart.

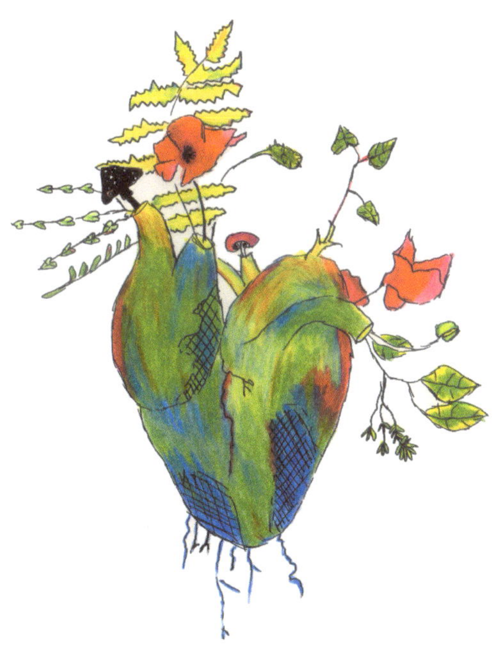

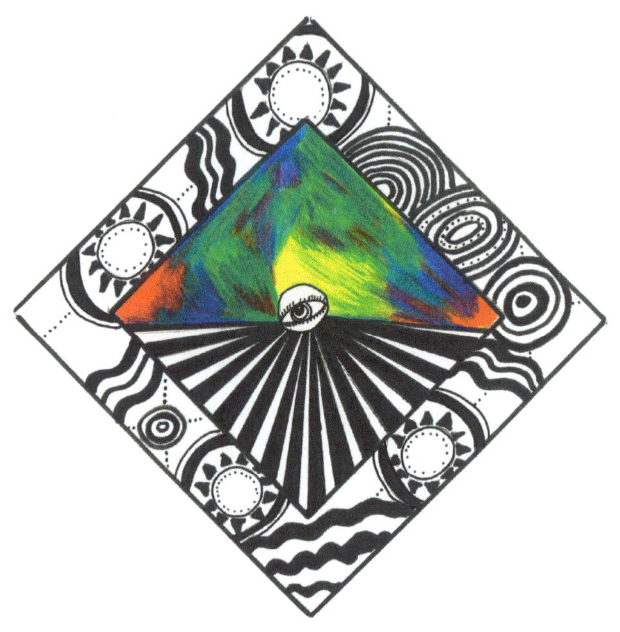

Inside the Falcons

About a kind of fig tree:
Ficus religiosa, an unbroken
line of devotion hiding bloom
inside its hollow, roots
dropped by birds, high into the canopy,
get the light you need to grow with vigor
then sending aerial shoots to the earth, thick and woody
encasing bark in a living mesh,
branches, matted strands of
hair featured in hymns, leafing myths
and seeds as embodied places of prayer,
immortal,
feeding belly and belief,
an intrigue for falcons
with little black
beaks.

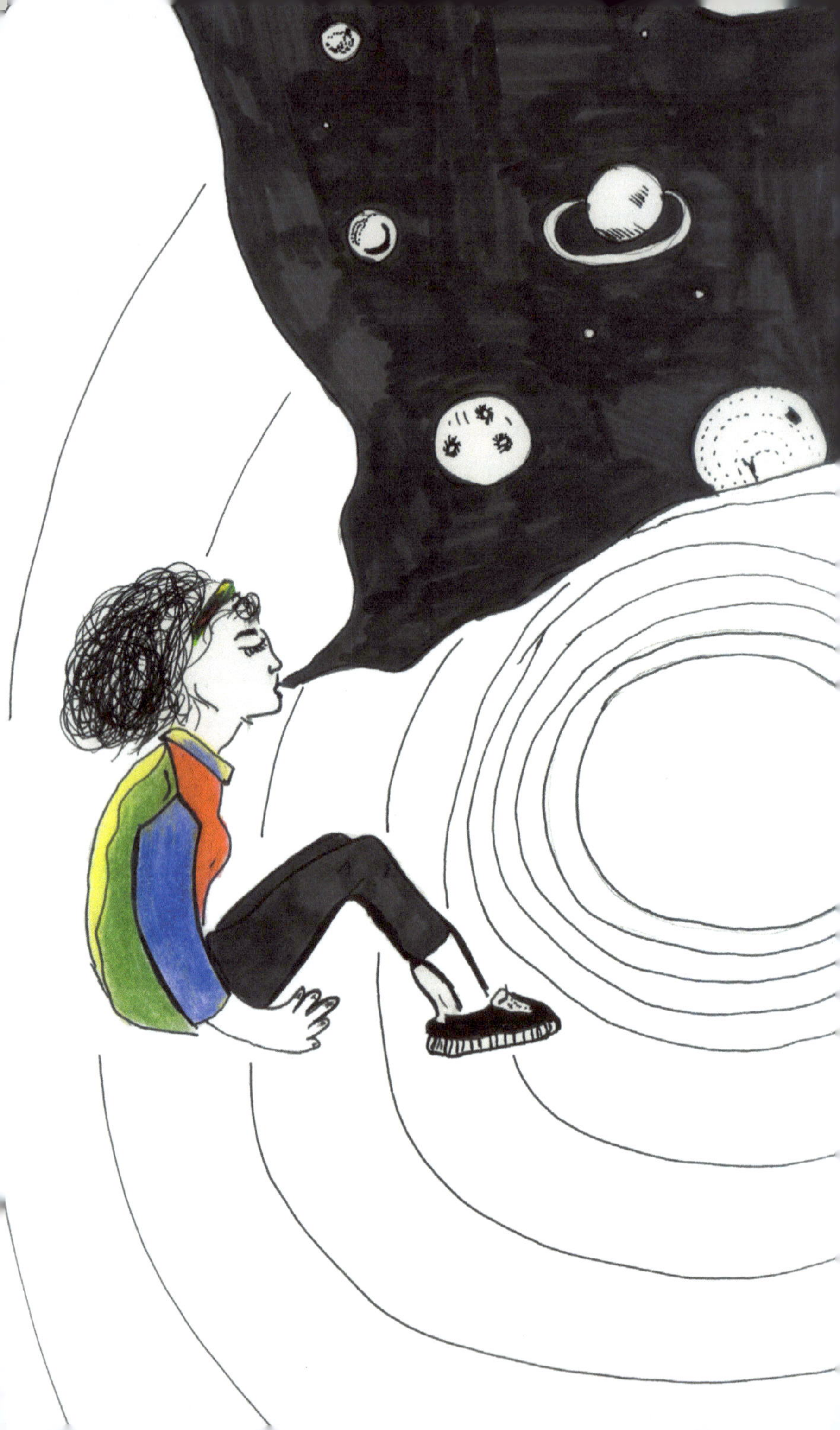

Refuge

huge stars appear
out of no where

while ancient tundras
crumble underneath our feet

a doorway to the under world
uncovers forests, carcasses and

200,000 years of thermokarst
growing deeper, no longer

shaded by summer mist,
we reach for

musk ox, mammoths,
and shelled molluscs,

jump into the spiraling
unknown.

In Site

I squeezed through the narrow
desert chasm
as time-worn winds battered the hills
and a terror struck,
speckled and eyes uncovered
in early spring

breath taking and carved into a valley
lined with pink
Oleander, hiked a seven thousand seat
theater up
to the sacrificial altar, geometric steps
and colonnades

neck-hewn tombs, herds of camels, a
few words in ancient script
behind the border guards, supersized
grins of *shukran*
(*thank you*) the crystal word,
kept reaching out,

giving just-ripe loquats to the north
and at the glacier,
baptism site where liquid light melts
in drowsy flow
I was found, a cradle of creation,
alive.

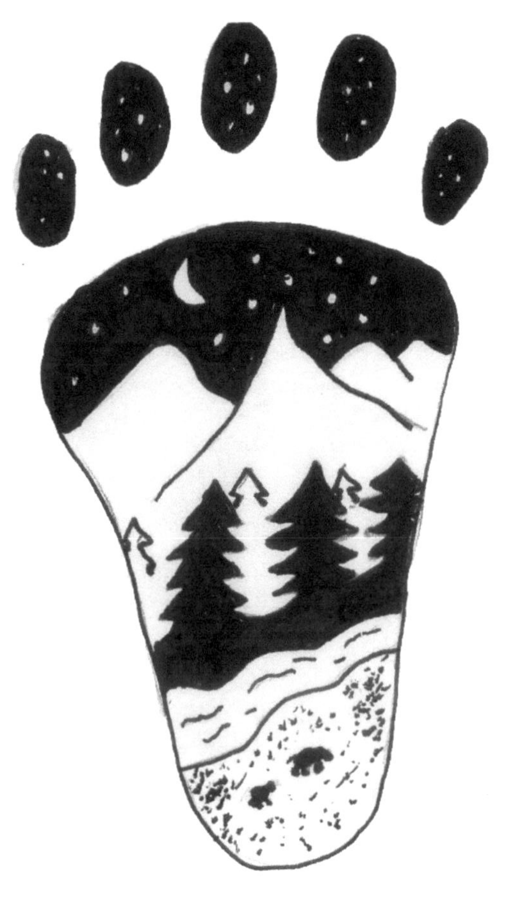

Whale Stranding of the Treemen

"In January, 29 sperm whales were found stranded on shores around the North Sea, an area that is too shallow for the marine wildlife."
– Press Mint News

high-powered sonar aimed at the bloom of desire
(you make my heart zone a whale stranding)

when currents push the whales inshore,
swearing bodies too sick to swim, un-earth

the false vibrations, short-circuit to the (heavenly) rocks
where sea creatures make

land
fall   to lay their eggs.

Few reach the spirals and sacred frequency of ocean
depths, thinking this   rise a safety secured

though standing in the break is the business
of abrasions, pouring gold into tunnels, the whale-

weight of bodies designed to adore the waters,
not bear their mass on land –

there is no crush in the gaze of a setting star
even if we die after being refloated   la petite mort

fishermen call the underwater branching
The Treeman Disease   gnarled as they are,

blossom hands and feet plumed in fear,
archers at dawn's first light

prohibitions in full gear,   pondering undercurrents,
pondering the flesh, skipping the holy precision

that tenders the somatic in space, passes through
sighs, splits beings into scintillating

specks,   a moment that ignites the sights, where moon
and sun meet to break the day—

remember the call of virgin Styx lethologica: a river
craving on the tip of the tongue

*(a chord, a drum-beat, a hip-swinging, finger-tapping
rhythm of color combinations)*

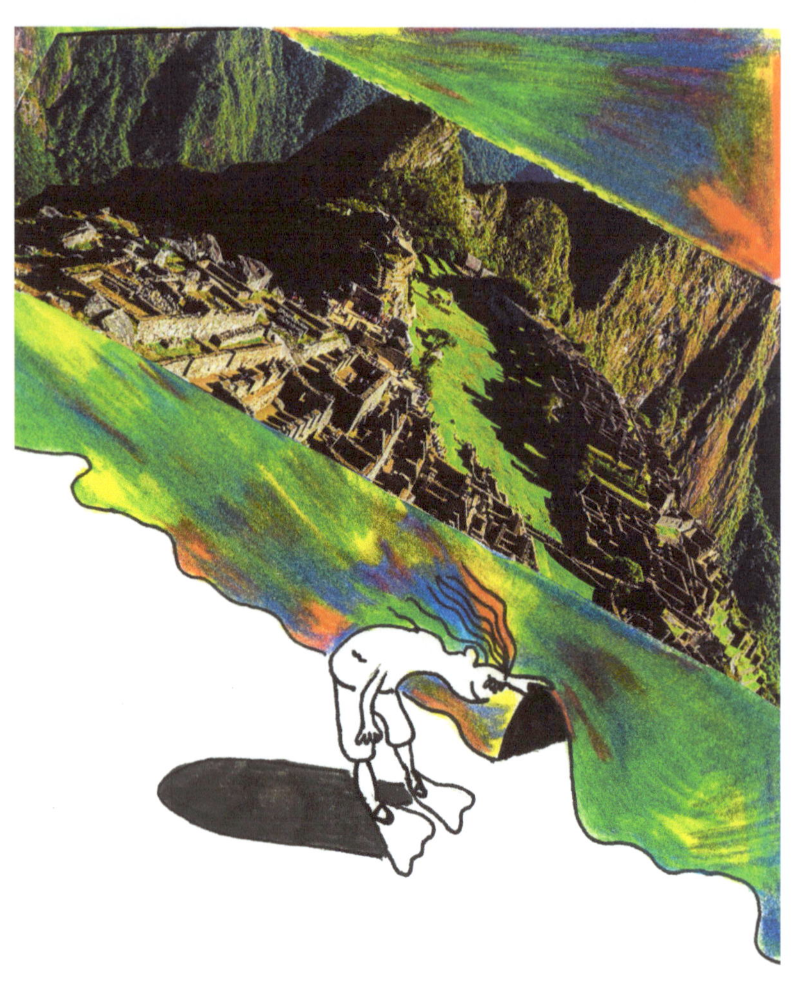

The Book of Miraculous Signs

Great Whale, Strange Beast,
you floundered amid the seas

there, falling from the sky
like a burning torch, a column,

a breakthrough and not a break
down

but still celestial beings wept,
filling calendars with the tears of moons

and unseen stars, a hailstorm that brought silence,
froze the earth, enveloped bodies with desire,

washing winds over all that stood in the way
until a new consciousness changed their colors,

saw you instead with a flower in your mouth
You could be a master of the air!

The Ballerina Project

young swallows succeeded
in breaching
the stereotype that the dance
form
was an art for the upper
class
only: despite dangers, the
ballerinas
took to the streets
in light
of restrictions imposed
by theaters,
institutions & halls, performing in the heavy
traffic
rain and garden attics, combining concrete
streets
with pink slippers
and skin,
eroding the parameters between outside/
in

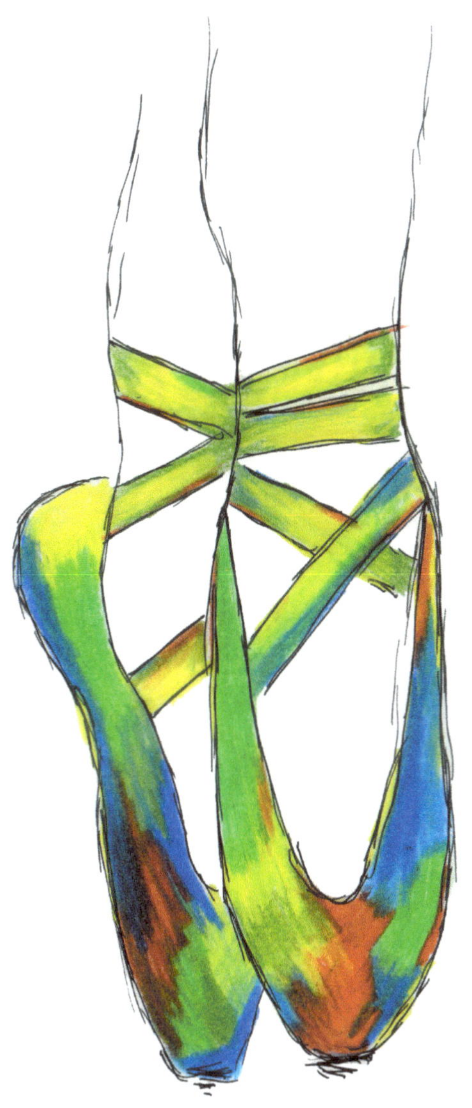

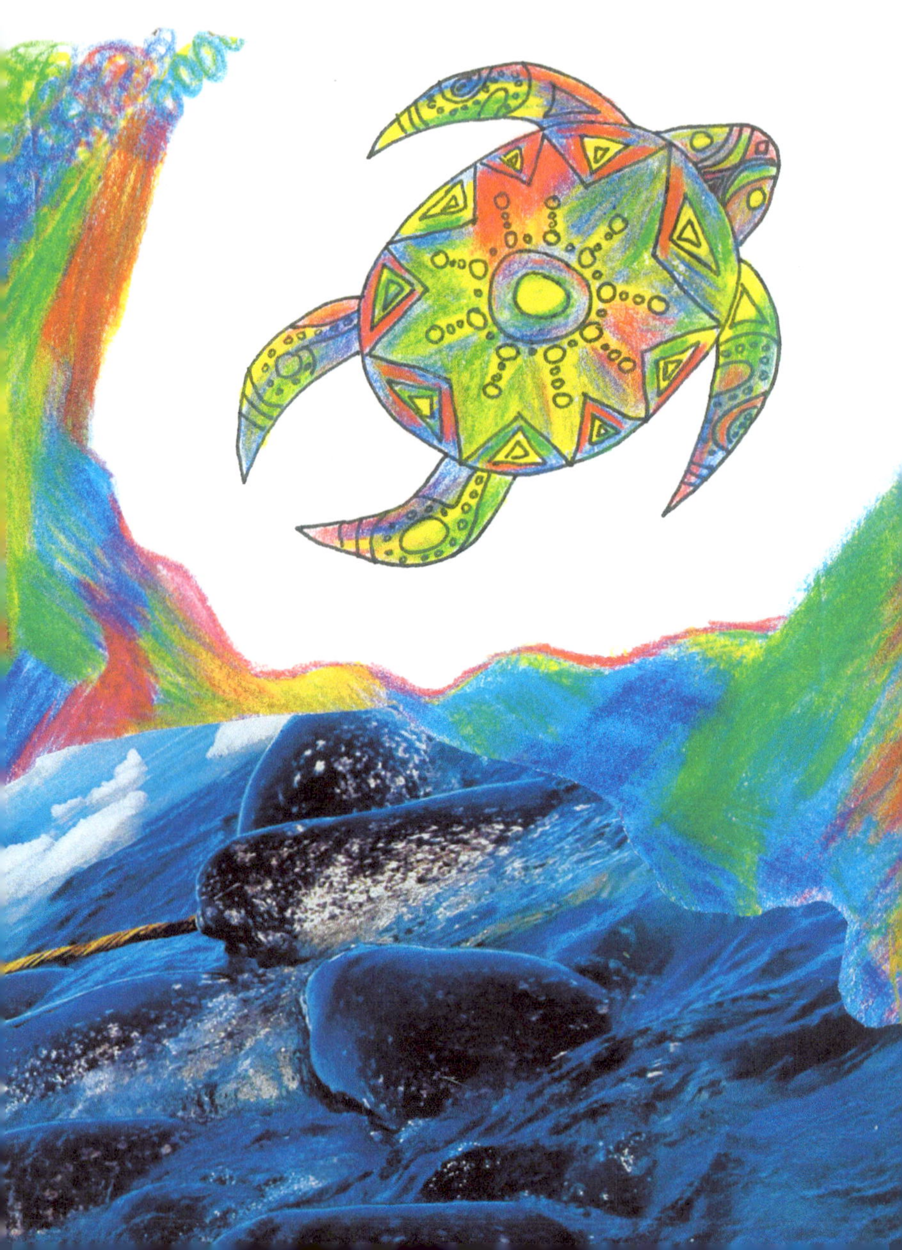

Pontiff

they told it as a lush, literate, epic
but it was more of a whalebone idea:
can I come closer to you?

you with bowels inhabited by wildlife
planted deep within,
the others with ghost-town hearts surrounded by sea

both ecosystems that lift and plunge

giant tortoise and seabirds, the edge

of an evolution that continues (to surprise) with life

marine iguanas foraging in the deep,
scraping the algae off rocks
gripping

so fiercely onto the sea floor
with claws that not even waves
can thrash them about.

Children in the Dust Valley

"In April, the Jordanian Ministry of Tourism revoked Mashrou' Leila's concert license, derailing a show planned at the Roman amphitheater in downtown Amman. Fans turned to the band's lyrics to express their defiance, sorrow and outrage on social media – and publications worldwide took note. Eventually, the ban was lifted, but not in time for the show to go on."
–NBC News

they come dressed in black star dust,
feet soaked in minerals,
arms extended like pedicels, catching dust
with caps they have made themselves

and with a sudden step, they grip wrestle
with nets out of water, break
the waves made of wire and time-glass with just one song
daring, bold font like white over tongues

star children tone *no missiles please,* for once
recite the selection you are burning,
blow up
the atoms for a peace of mine

ballrooms fill with rebels hot on wine
boot the brown that roots the mud of the holy land
when bodies not themselves echo the loud of prayers
(torn)

orbits of the Loon reach for the bright
that knows de-fogging
feuds among the warlords weeping
in their beds at night, the amphitheater is empty tonight

but silence has gone to sleep,
we have known
symphonies that frame the fires
and rage that doesn't b/

reak swallowing our secrets whole,   spin the crash
body of a flood
flushing the genealogy of rise and west, the east
and set, the climbers, the peaks, the patterns, the fall-

shattered   pink   and   blue-   fathers born
to rear sons
as hawks
and iris mothers, once blinded in monochrome

call in the music   of lampshade furs and graffiti,
play a shadow-tuning of the night, the rhythm of star
children   honeyed inside
the hive, buzzing a new dimension.

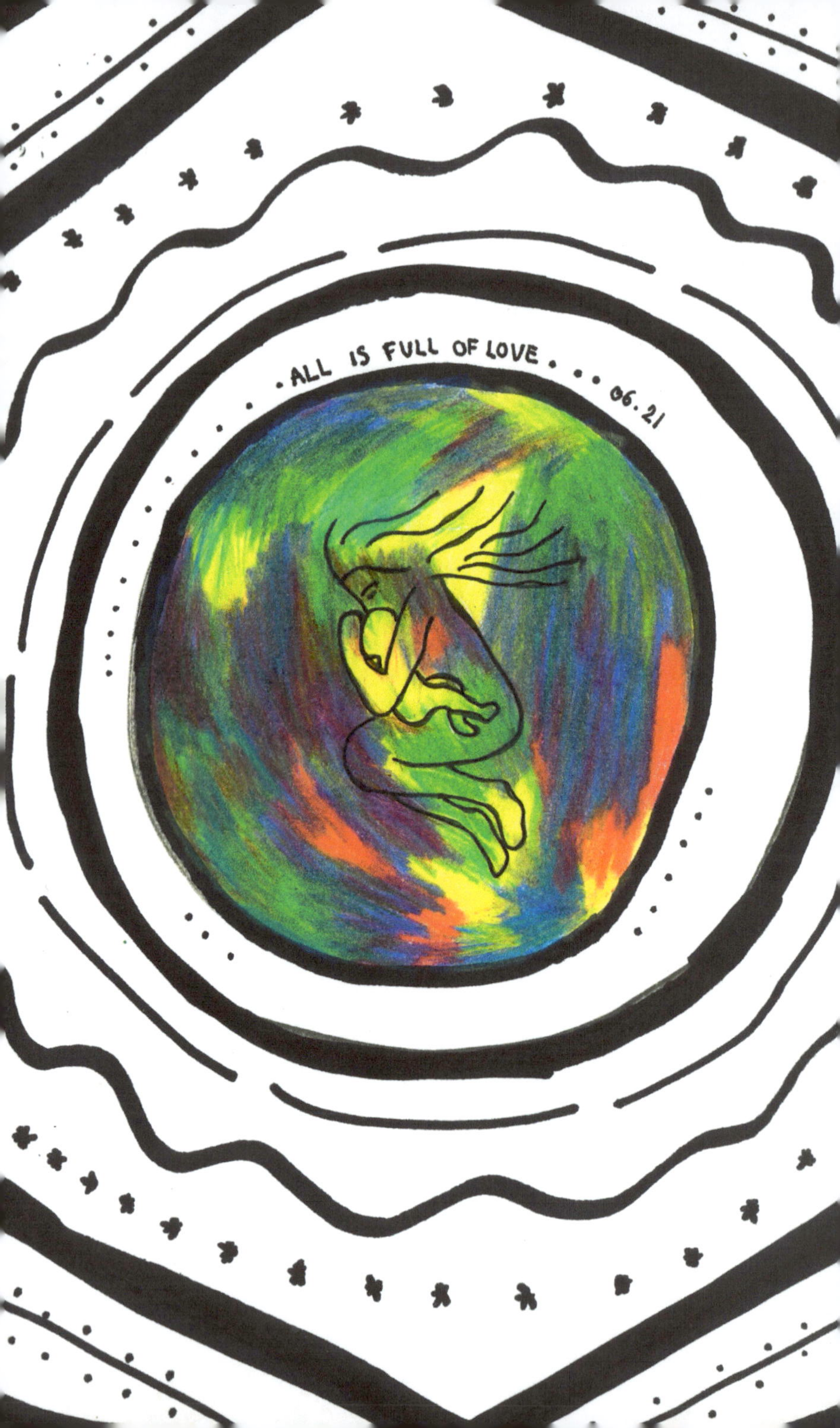
ALL IS FULL OF LOVE
06.21

Mesentery

an organ long thought
to be made up of fragments,
separate and scarred new
impulses show it as one continuous
perception, a double fold of peritoneum
cormorant flavor-lining the
cavity that keeps everything
locked in place the way da Vinci
sketched velvet waistcoats and pipe
smoke, the way textbooks swallow more
than anatomy and structure, the function
of black pebbles is to sense handsels alive
within our bodies, rising and falling as if
in slow
motion.

Moonwalk

I might have been somewhere close when Apollo entered
the lunar orbit of freedom fighters, freelance writers,
portraits of bike riders carrying forts along their arms

gazing at the moon-filled tokens

wild rogues gathering around the fire *exhale*
a gravitational pull equal to the frequency of your desire,
rewind for the compensation of a proximity that scales

the senses, sends you on a pleasure trip around the world!

Gravity

the glass-winged creature enters through
the window to watch
your dissection of the grotesque—its eyes
stride across the doorway,
delight at the gentle outpouring of faith (a
conflict within the self that unravels,
lungs
opening
like an   aperture,
charging the cracks with chimera)
it reads the energy of your celestite, your
lashes, watches   the reel
reveal
whispers of the albatross   they draw
in
its wayfaring
ebb.

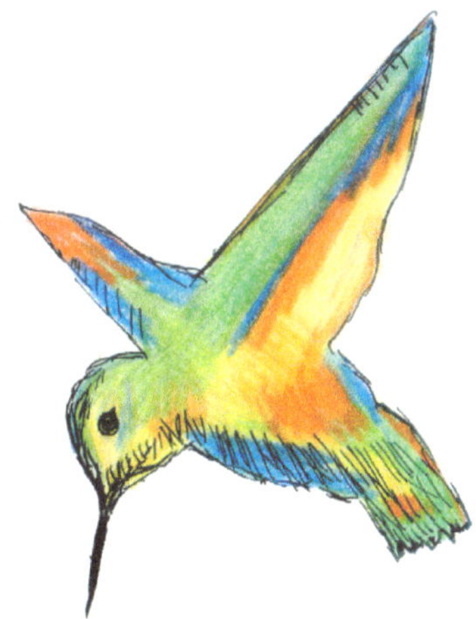

Call of the Orca

We believe in the large mass between us that curves space-time,
distorts its fabric, in whale—gravity at its strongest,
drawing the tides out of the cetacean
heart, landmarks

the morning's coffee lips, raw
curiosity against the cracks
excavating a sublime vibration
merging pupils, iris, lens
windows   into a never-before realized
opened   bright even at the slight of a cigarette puff of

ground zero   in the search for gravitational waves
ground zero   in the search for the subjects that produce them
ground zero   the most energetic, wild, and interesting
    moments in the universe

  where myth weavers
      break   the monotony,
      a non-combat mission in the drought-hit Somalia
      of the modern soul caught upon borders
      and ceremonial roles
      offering guards in black hats, cuffs, and boots (gorilla
      gates of tradition) manikins of waste
      collecting fumes and saccharine laws
      it is not about hugging trees,
      but tackling the unscheduled topics,
                                    knowing exploration
      that fires the pulse and veers towards
      the construction of a fusion reactor
      alley swing of the world's first

      underwater

      museum:

hear the blue cartridge call of the Orca,

dip a toe

into the infinite waters

of the see.

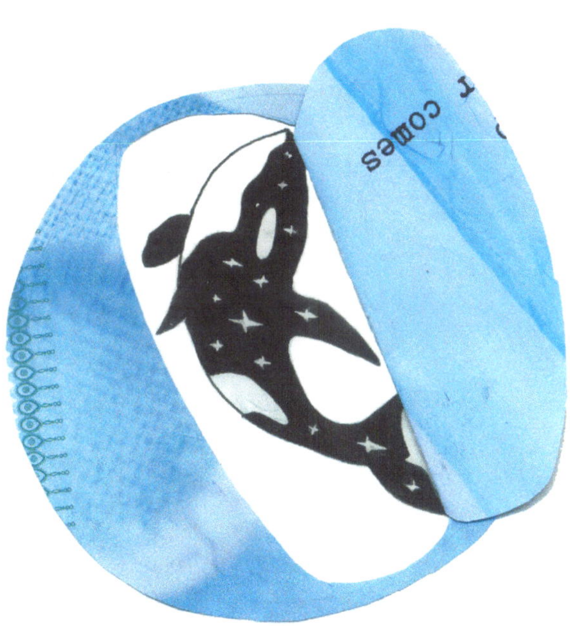

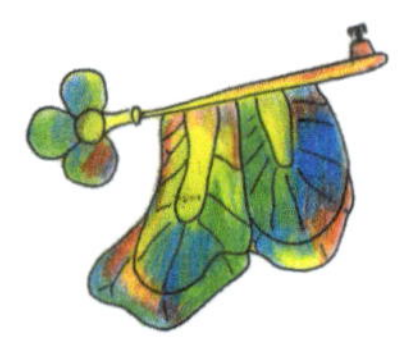

Footnote

a butterfly molecule explodes: this
weak
pairing of excitable
atoms
confirms the existence of a new type of
bond
created when electrons are kicked
far
from an atom's nucleus, common
enough
(on their own) now attract, bind segments of soul
to sun
(something thought impossible) charm
moon-eyed atoms,
pulling them into their arms, notice changes in the frequency
of light
molecules with the capacity to absorb
oil fields,
peaks and valleys on fire, pry you
open
your heart is just
reverberating
secrets in here somewhere, there's always more to
gravity,
always in the present
tense
always an embryo making space in the body where there was
none
(all else is footnote).

Radio Transmission

Startled as when I first heard the star-music
like a radio transmission at a gas stop
unexplained sounds tend to do that—
make us mistake moonlight for a snake-rattler

nature's broadcast, a tremor from the far side of the rock
rippling
as though it understood
the courtship of light

from that place behind the clouds where crafts fall out of
contact—scattering,
a hush and spin as lines curl into a constellation,
dive into that strange-seduction,

a silence that sheds coats,
sings flesh
and foam onto bones
(facts spell *the taste of skin is peach*)

a flowering that whistles the tune
to an ancient audio event ...
the sight of fledglings
on the horizon

we signaled for mission control
but it was a message
too large to pin
down.

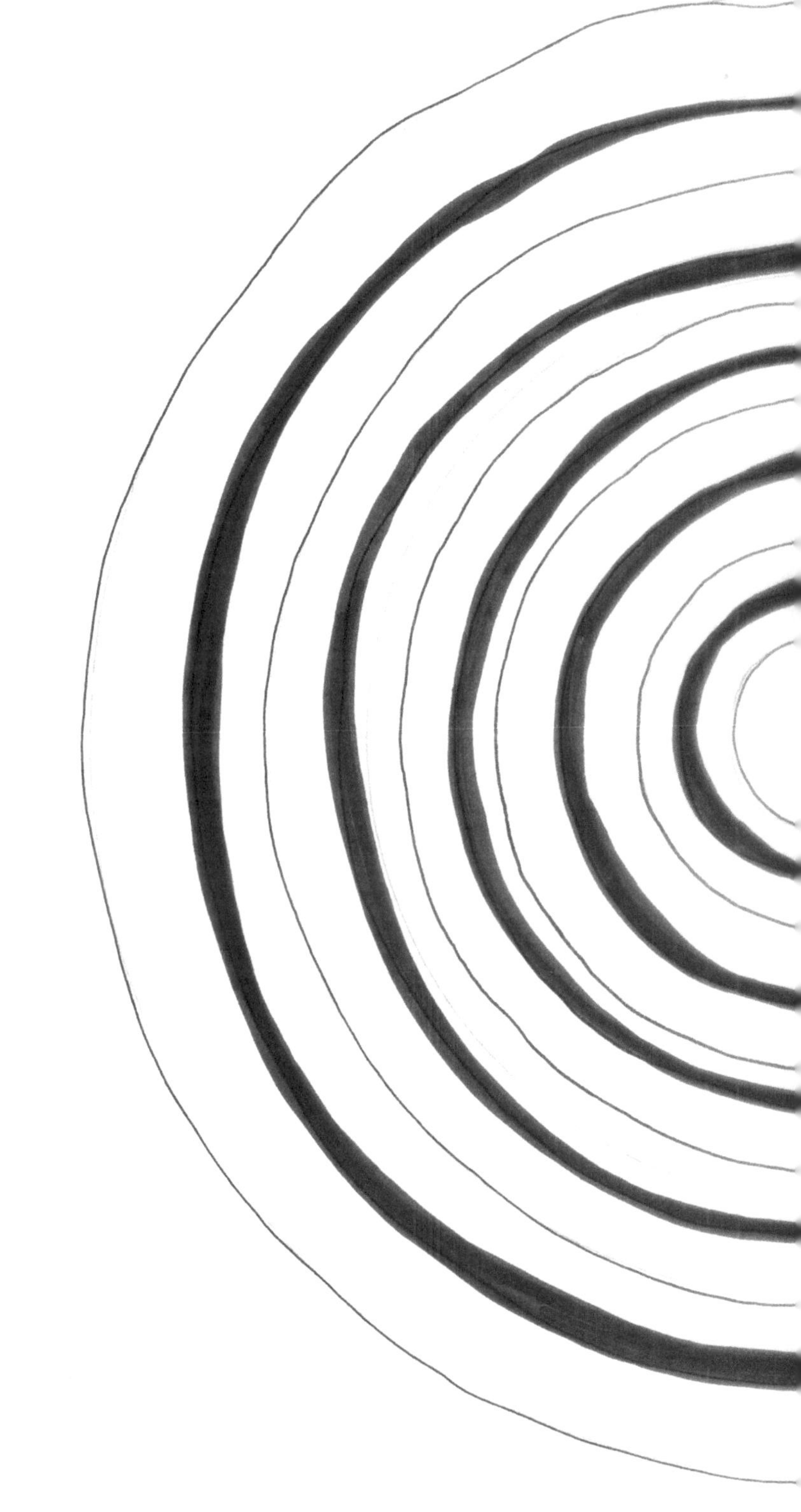

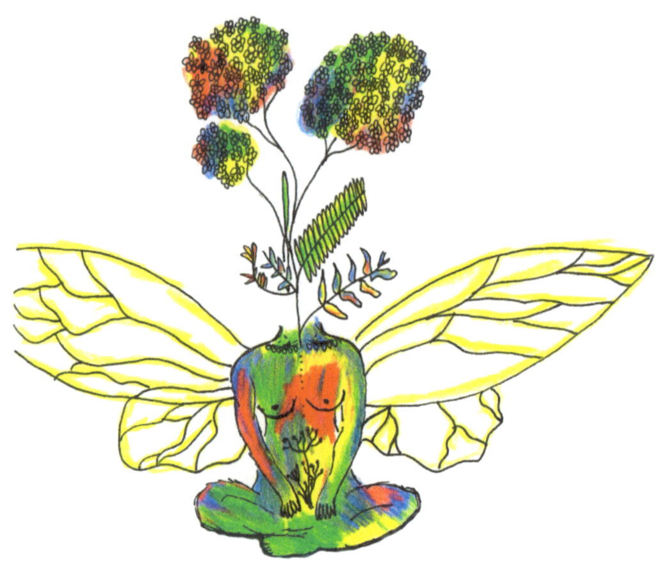

Waves

"qu'est-ce-que vous desirez?" the stranger asks
and out of trivialities we walk into the blazing light,
chariot-race against the laps ...

I'm not sure what it means
but these colors move me
and the sun carries me to safety,
unhooks the tame,
tunes to the core of the whale ... *listen closely*
(the sea's laughter ripples across the empires)

we carry each other over the water, bathe our heads
in the tendering waves, dive into the heartening trenches
and every winter morning, we touch the inscriptions
as if each l e t t e r contained
an antidote to this sickness,

prayer flags dancing as autumn mourns
the thousand year old death of a lunar spell.
We awakened the giants of Central Asia,
replaced the eye of the Cyclops, so dim was he
that history penned him
in (weaving from the shadows he sang)

and so the real voyage continued
and with our beautiful companions by our side
the unusual music of the moon found us kneeling
by a temple of light.

Entangled System

when the lightening strikes
states change unimaginably
quickly,
gaze and tongue absorbed
by the current

or softly distributed among many
fields, a stream that lasts
in attoseconds
(or zeptoseconds even),
oscillating inside the bark,

water chips into Nabatean rock
and soon, eyes feast on soaring
arches, a luster born out of
everything (we thought)
we saw
and how we came to seal it.

Reimagined

In the desert metropolis where the summer
is long and shade, a shiny metal canopy,

mirrors rounded the motorways, angled
to reflect galleries of enlightenment,

a seed vault much like a field of sunflowers
or a new take on the 70s disco ball (but hushed),

uttering patterns, spelling out words, parading
a new way to play with soap, sun, and light levels.

It Ends With Beauty

stunted: short and
a sign of malnutrition
splitting bread into smaller
rations and the situation
worsens or Aleppo rages
or the brink of famine in Yemen:

a window through which to glimpse
this bamboo-clad patch of mountains
we believed we were a breed
apart, small and unchanging
quartz,
black holes, particles

of light, multiform and (boundless)
burials coated in sound,
unexpected vibrations
in a region ablaze, fire-stretching
were we so hungry to begin with?
swallowing sunsets

when illuminated
feathers
dropped
over
the
orchestra.

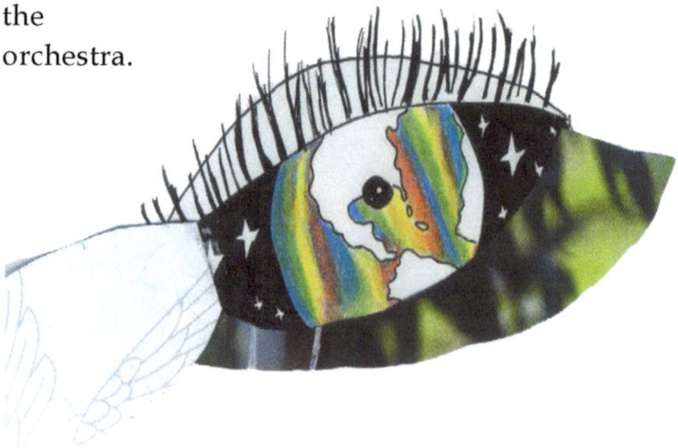

Gross National Happiness

Fireworks light up the sky over the capital:

a prince is born and to celebrate, the people

have planted trees

one hundred and eight thousand

seeds each sealed

with a wish for their heir

May you live a savage life
and bring peace to your kingdom.

May your love soak the land
like a monsoon.

May you grow to be strong as the Carob trees
and kind as the kindest eyes that move the deep of every

human
sea –

night clocks the electric dreams,
drives them through the capital's heart.

Mother's Prayers

Saint of the Gutter Trance
Feeding the poorest of the poor,
We live in the soul of a city

No room for complacency when hunger
For love, you say
Is so much more difficult (to remove)

Than hunger for bread; she heals
Men who call caves their home
With prayers (openings through which

The sun beams weave) lush jungles
Down the side of serrated cliffs
The shrill call of birds and macaque

Monkeys echoing off the limestone
Drifting in from the unseen world
Beyond the skylight, or what we called

This place when we first discovered it
Forms and foam tied up and thrown
To the bottom

Of the calm
Silver
Sea.

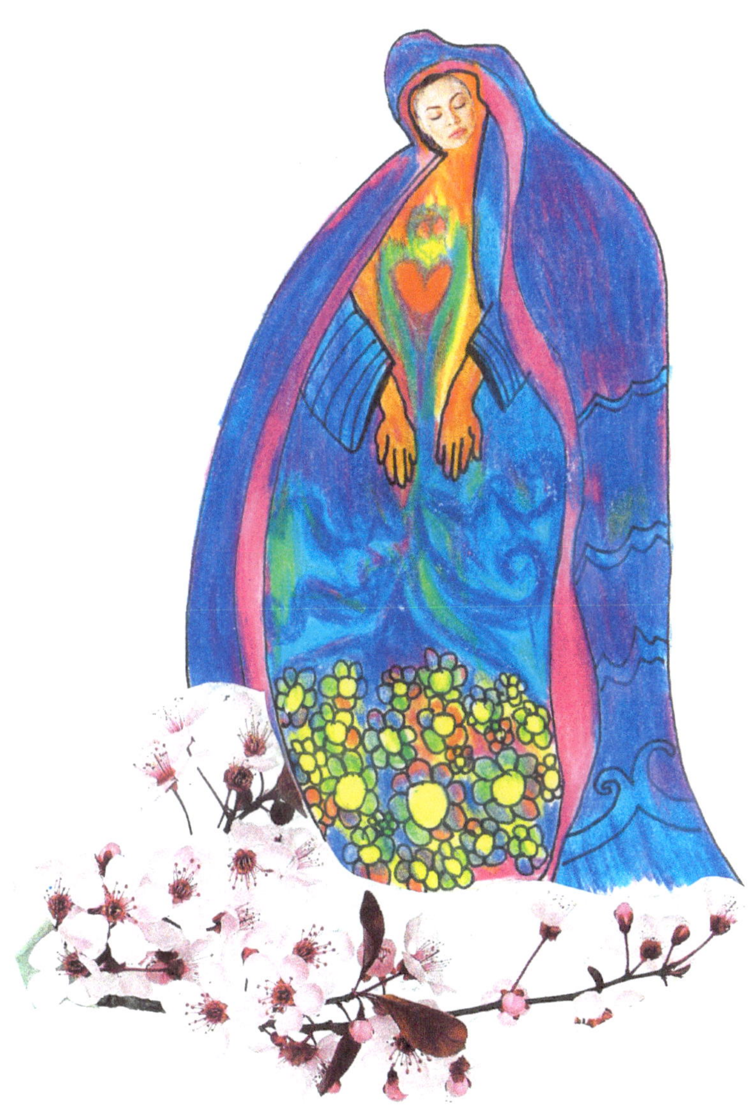

Marine Assemblage

divers discover a treasure trove
a sixteen hundred year old shipwreck,
bronze statues and thousands
(of coins) a lamp depicting Sol the sun
god, a figurine of the moon goddess
Luna, and objects in the shape of animals,
a whale, a wild boar with a swan
on its head—exciting finds with more than
beauty to account for their charge.

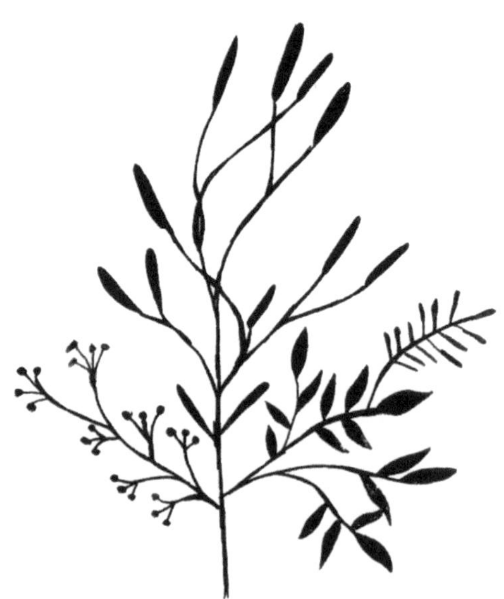

Hesitations of History

"natural allies" (a term discarded
in the years since) we hit the right
buttons

comfort and convergence
defined our conversations, an instinct to
turn beef-barriers into booklets

mealy-mouthed, our collage ensouled
a luminous island, a garment of glaze
like fabled reefs, a folk frequency loud

and effervescent, then block.   that seemed
insurmountable until we came undone;
a voyage or shield unsealed.

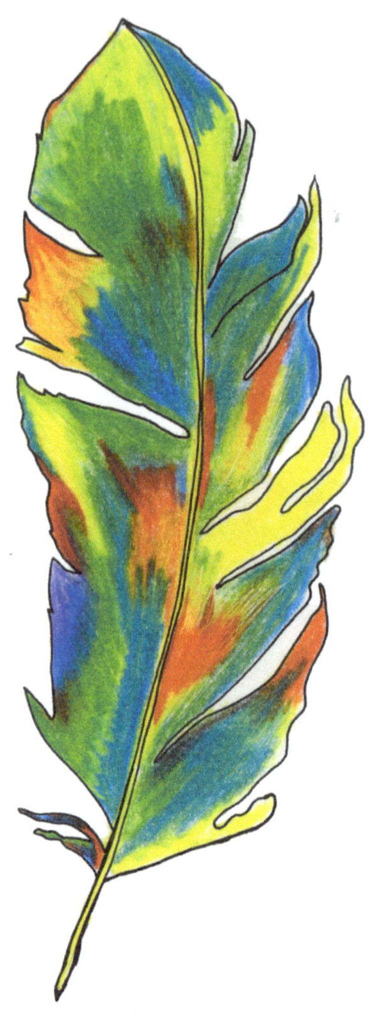

The Way of the Lover

We hold the story of you by the hand,
its wrinkled skin bearing revelations,
bearing light amplified and dewy desires
wrapped in a silence that thaws,
lay them down by the feet of the anchoring shore,
lay them alongside the battle that is your tenderness,

we see these oceans as a reflection,
no more separation in the space
(between us) there is only Now—
now where all the waves crash and unfold,
inside every rock and rippling lake,
raw feeling like an uncut diamond

we sense you inside and out
you and your once jittery pulse
now melting from within this sea of loving, welcoming
cells into a house of being where there is nothing Other,
a Beloved who is also Beloving,
the beloving in us, a state and mirror of it all.

Eclipse on the Perfect Island

the information included the diamonds'
snow grammar of intimacy, the pebbled light that plants
can taste, the photosynthesizer's turning of oxy and bright
into sugar sweet specks of night.

we flock to witness the rare celestial event, currency
tucked in the sleeves of our neon eyes, a perfect desert
island with no names to feed the pores, just a fringe of
palm trees against the backdrop of a dense, unexplored
~~forest~~ ocean
ask the right questions and the sky unfolds as a migratory
corridor for rays, turtles, pelagic fish, dolphins, whale
sharks and humpbacks (a thrilling place to dive)
this wide is still
a milky lilac,
showers us with lemon and timebefore curling out into the

drop and fly of darknessleaving only a skyline of
cashmere
hands soclose charge of waves on skin like
chrysanthemums painted in the
clearest
hues on earth, reflected on our patch of desert, we hear
things only meant to be touched by the
moon (just
broad enough to cover her solar twin) she offers midnight
as the perfect habitat for
our perfect ~~mouths~~

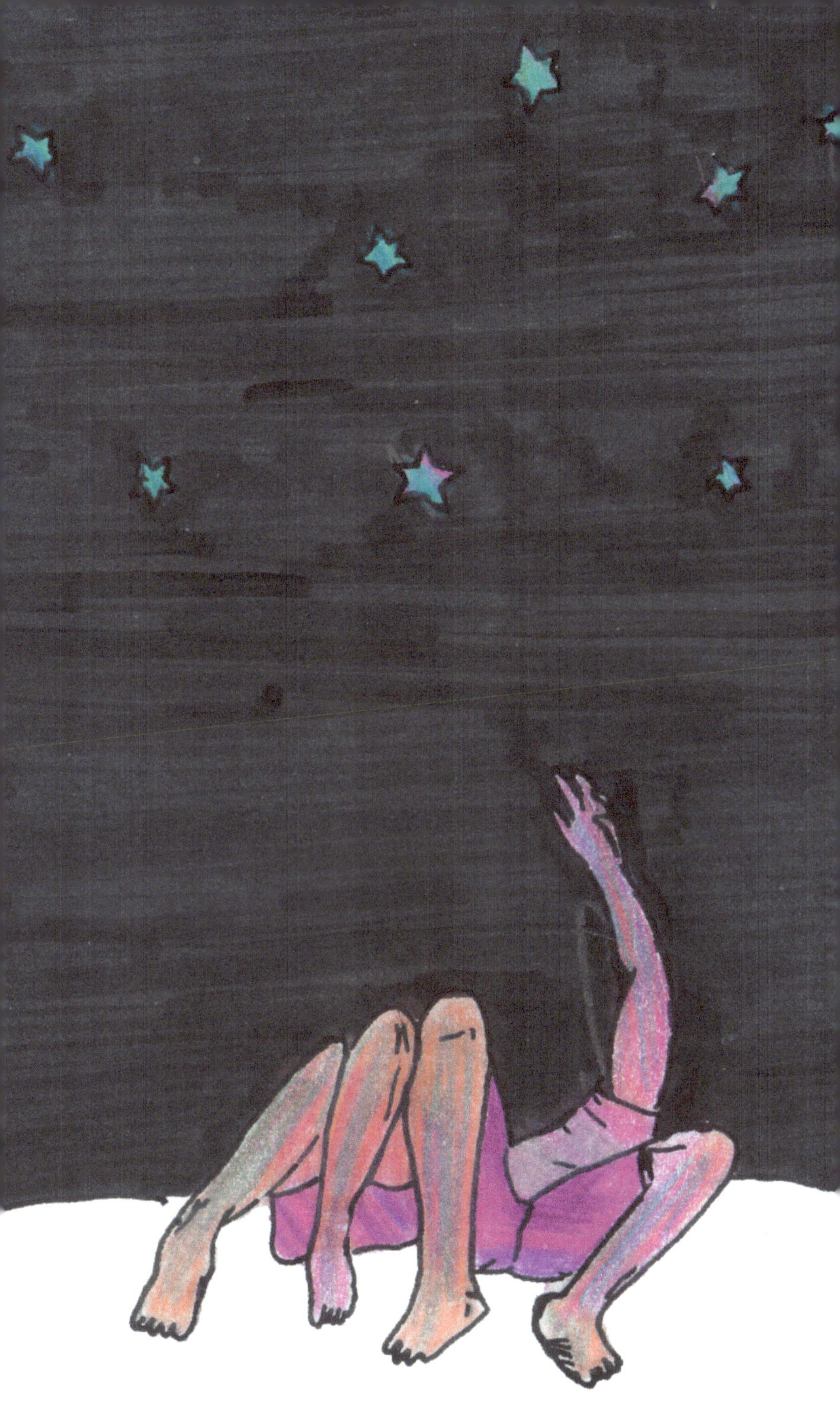

When a Telescope

first finds a moving object
all we know is it's a dot
lashing through the sky,
whizzing past Earth tonight
no metrics spelled the distance
or range
or color
like phosphorus.

the more telescopes pointed, the more
data was unburied, the more we saw
the burning into bones,
how big it was, how beautiful
(the way it trails as a fall)
though sometimes we don't have
the time to make firm observations,
a rain of fire, a whole incendiary city on fire.

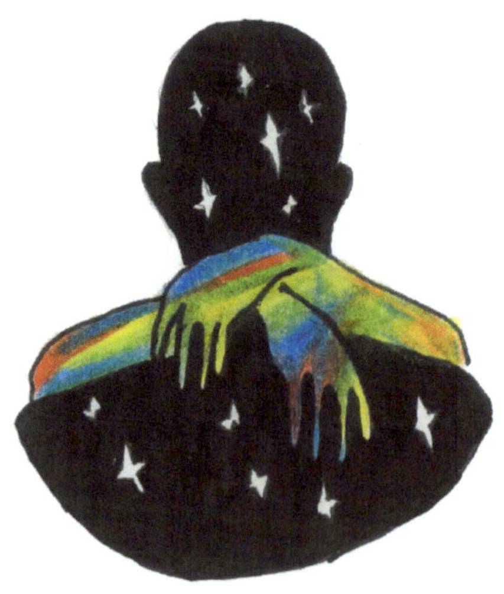

The Lost Voices of Petra

sunbirds bounce   off
the towering sandstone
cliffs   as we hike through
the narrow canyon, the low
angle of morning paints
red and gold the cloak
of Babylon on the
surrounding lands, intricate
channels, pools supplying
the city with running
waters, past the Flintstones
House, past the temples
and tombs, past petroglyphs
with their own clues,
centuries before time then
vanished into mountainsides,
an iconic view and the scent
of incense and clove,
a mishmash of elements
as a breeze travels
into the heart
look up at the sun
the talk
of angels
and other worlds
are scribbled
in this light.

I Walked Across Because

the woman ambled thousands of miles from Siberia
to the holy continent, seven countries, eight pairs
of walking boots, thirteen years, three thousand
cups of tea to understand the cryptic codes of wildlife
and what I'm made of
on a basic level
she boarded across lands made of honey and wine,
ending the journey under a tree
in the desert where wolves came
howling around my tent
an adventure inside of us belonging
to the earth,
the inaudible music that moves us
along in our bodies.

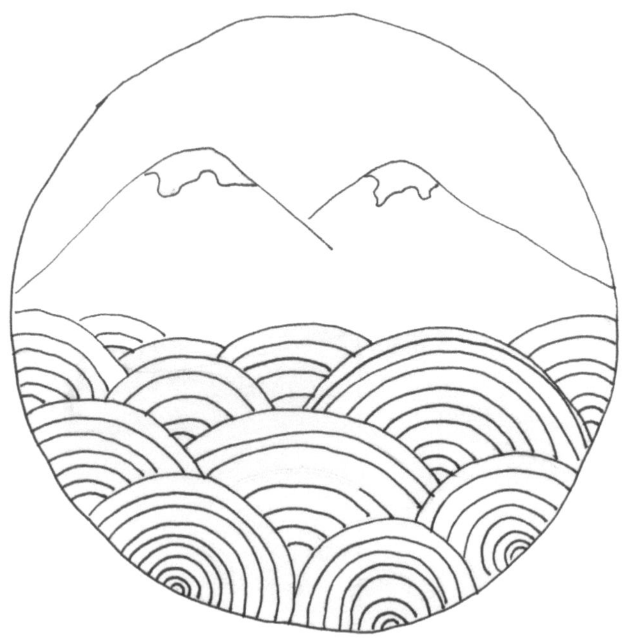

The Most Important Fossil You've Never Heard of

not a household name, but a lost creature
how four-limbed I was, became established on land
then, an animal found inside rocks, a backbone
a pair of lungs and five fingers

small-step-giant-leap became
birds, dinosaurs, crocodiles, mammals, lizards
then, another step   and no longer imprisoned
within

the narrow compass
of skulls,
yesterday Tiny remained
trapped in a rock, hidden from view

now she follows the dirt road leading to the mountain
where I walk, barefoot and bright
between the sandstone cliffs
bending my way out of the woods, rounding into the heart

of the third see

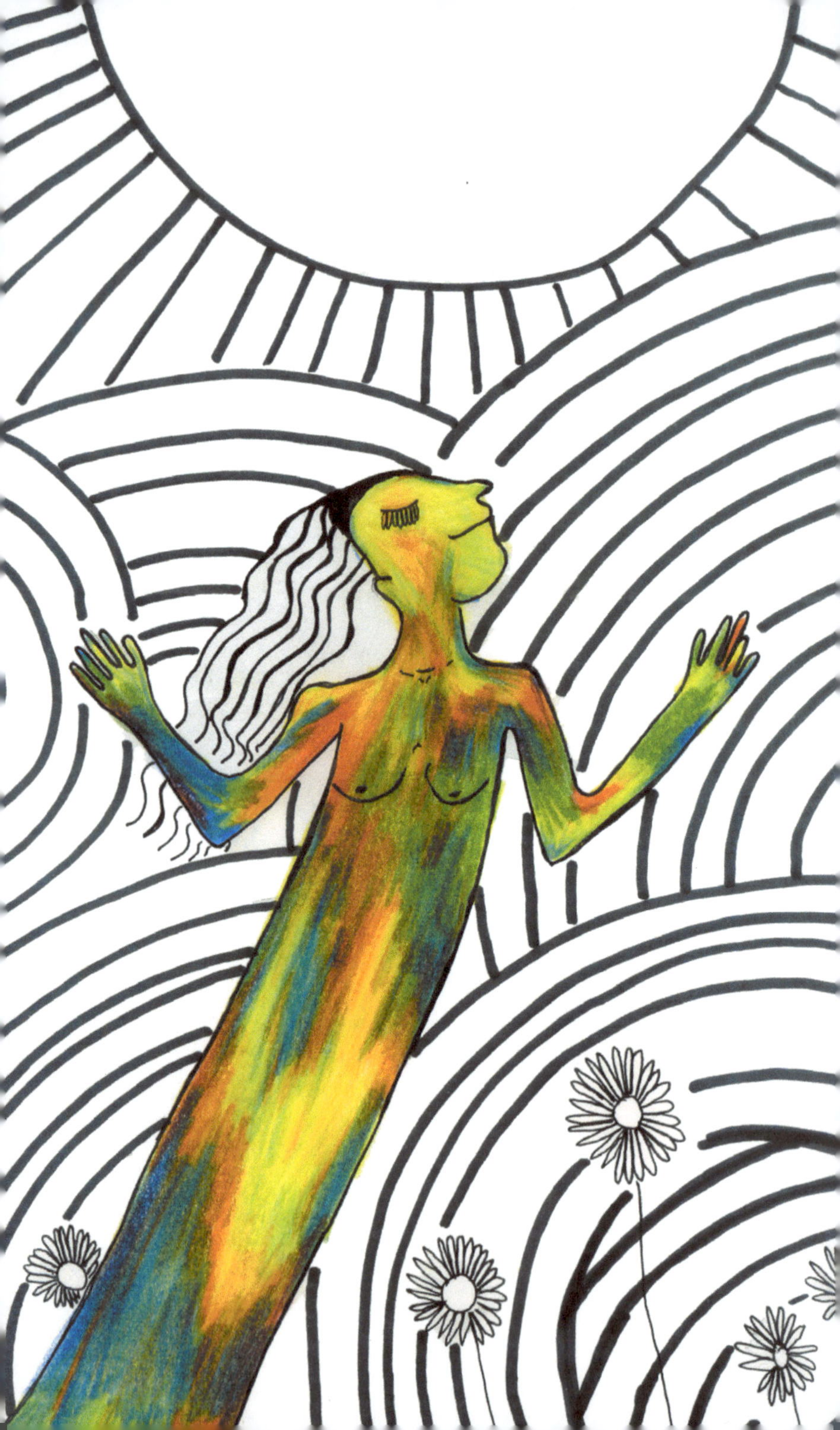

The World's Smallest Kingdom

The lonely island rose wildly
from the sea
like a jagged mountain

the only inhabitable stretch
a white sand-tongue
measured in steps

she commanded this mini-
monarchy in a robe of roses, daughter
of the waters and the world's most earthy queen

ribs stretched out in grass, mountains and leaves
wild-goat views (and teeth
dyed a golden-yellow by lichen)

a sunheart wires
her shrubs and mudflats to the frequency
of~~———Imagination———~~illumination

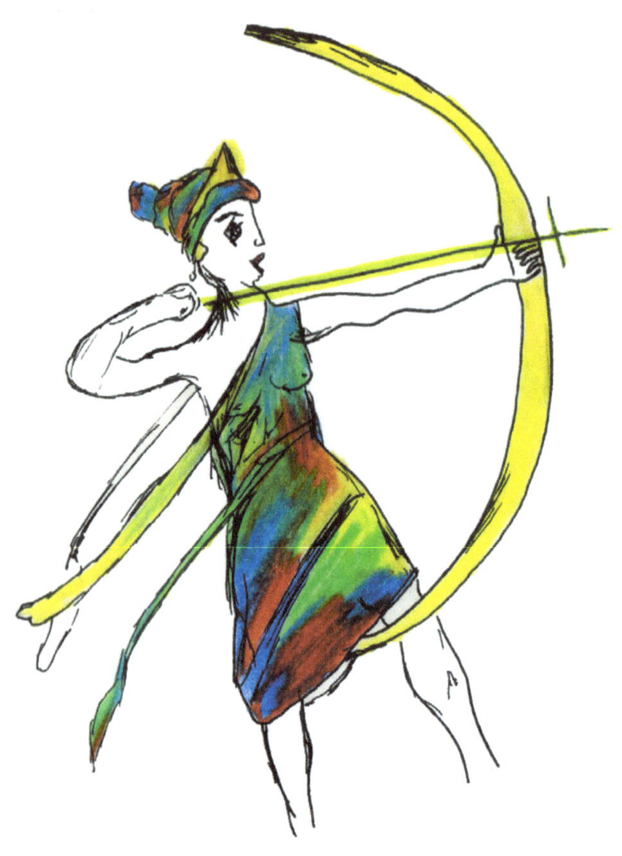

North

in search of a true-nature tribe
the proper study of man became everything
a hot hidden Africa, a colonial playground
except bullet-proof like sugar spring and lips
lined with logic and maps
tasks, deadlines, gadgets, whole constellations tuned
without a whisper of
here and honey

and wholly
this "Made in Dreams"
said everything blown
phantasmagoric

I laughed and lingered on softer space and sea.
You plugged in frowns, mumbles, a fear
of firsts and feathers that injures
as though to say something like *cloudcandy* was insult
to the far off sky

not the fencing (of the earth)
but silk embrace and sun-moons that siren and swallow
in chanting chambers. *Feel free*
to fade (you ask who needs words)
I say let them fall always   on what is true and hold
that note because there is
no other
way.

www.ingramcontent.com/pod-product-compliance
Lightning Source LLC
LaVergne TN
LVHW052256100826
845147LV00001B/60

* 9 7 8 1 9 3 6 6 7 1 6 1 8 *